BUILDING LITERACY
WITH
INTERACTIVE CHARTS

A Practical Guide for Creating 75 Engaging Charts
from Song, Poems, and Fingerplays

by Kristin G. Schlosser and Vicki L. Phillips

S C H O L A S T I C
PROFESSIONAL BOOKS

NEW YORK • TORONTO • LONDON • AUCKLAND • SYDNEY

Dedicated to the children of Allison Elementary School,
who are the greatest teachers of all.

—K.S.

To Mom, who always encouraged me to read and create.

—V.P.

ACKNOWLEDGMENTS
● ● ● ● ● ● ● ● ● ● ● ● ● ●

This book would not have been possible without the help and support of many people. I am grateful to the following people who graciously shared their materials, time, ideas, and support: Diana Moran, Kay Neal, Kathy Weber, Diane Beckham, Priscilla Dunn, Amy Kacarab, Terry Ruben, Mary Roberts, Karen Eads, and Karen Bryant. Surely these are the greatest teachers that a child could have, and I feel honored to have collaborated with them. To all, a heartfelt thank you.

—K.S.

Special Thanks to the Following: Arlitt Child Development Center, University of Cincinnati, for their commitment and contributions to the education of young children; Deb Rudolph, Paula Hoeffer, and Karen Bryant for sharing their charts, ideas, and talents; Jen Crowe and Amanda White for help with photography; and all the children in my classes, whose enthusiasm and literacy growth have provided me with insight and inspiration.   —V.P.

Design by Jacqueline Swensen
Cover Design by Vincent Ceci
Interior Illustration by Teresa Anderko
Photographs by Jen Crowe and Amanda White
Copyright © 1992 by Scholastic Inc. All rights reserved.

ISBN 0-590-49234-9

12 11 10 9 8 7 6 5 4 3   4 5/9

Printed in the U.S.A.

Thanksgiving Day

The _____ ran away

Before Thanksgiving Day.

He said, "They'll make

a _____ of me

If I decide to stay."

- -

Children draw a tiny picture to illustrate each of the word cards below and cut them out. Fold this paper up on the dotted line.
Staple the sides to create a pocket. Store word cards in the pocket.

turkey	roast	cranberry
sauce	pumpkin	pie

Table of Contents

Foreword 4

Introduction 6

Interactive Charts: Questions and Answers 7

Name Charts 13

Seasonal Charts 23

Number Charts 37

Functional Print Charts 47

Thematic Charts 53

Charts Related to Literature 69

Recommended Sources for Interactive Chart Texts 80

Foreword

My first experience with interactive charts was during a kindergarten education course at the University of Cincinnati. Dr. Diane Blackburn, a front runner in the whole language movement, assigned each class member the task of creating and displaying an interactive chart. I vividly recall my search for an appropriate poem, the consideration I put into the design of the chart, and the time I spent in the process of creation. The best part of the assignment was when all the participants shared their charts. With great enthusiasm, I copied all the ideas to add to my growing arsenal of intended charts.

Interactive charts seemed to be the perfect bridge between whole language theory and practice. I knew that they were child-centered, visually attractive, and based on oral language. Interactive charts gave children the opportunity to manipulate and interact with print in a concrete way and transferred their oral language knowledge to written form. With all this in mind, I felt I had the key to unlocking the mysteries of emerging literacy and was now ready to begin my new teaching assignment as a kindergarten teacher.

I carefully wrote nursery rhymes on sentence strips and provided a duplicate copy for the children to match to the text. I placed them thoughtfully throughout the classroom. After waiting anxiously for the children to begin making the oral/written connection, I was sadly disappointed. But, knowing that interactive charts were based on sound research, I began to re-evaluate and re-create charts with a few valuable alterations. I learned many things about interactive charts that first year.

I discovered that children increase their interaction with charts if they are based on a familiar poem, song, or fingerplay with lots of child appeal. The children should first learn the chart orally for enjoyment before the teacher introduces its written counterpart. I rediscovered the powerful effects of modeling. Children need to see the teacher using interactive charts many times. Lastly, I learned that flooding the classroom with unfamiliar print was overwhelming. Instead, I now put fewer, familiar, and frequently modeled charts throughout the classroom. We always start our day with singing or reciting an interactive chart together.

I also learned that children need variety. When all my charts consisted of matching the sentences, the children lost interest. However, the children now use a variety of formats with great enthusiasm. I discovered too the impact of charts that include the child's name. This personal touch assures instant popularity for the chart and increases the children's interaction with letters and sounds. Many children learn letter discrimination and recognition through using name cards, such as discriminating between BRIAN and BRITTANY.

I have also learned many valuable lessons about creating and choosing material for interactive charts. "The Farm Song," which is pictured below, is one example of a poor choice for my classroom. Because this was a popular song with the children, I decided to use it as the basis for an interactive chart. Unfortunately, the chart turned out to be less effective than I had envisioned. It was oversized and had too many manipulable components. The cumbersome process of attaching the manipulable parts detracted from the enjoyment and meaning of the song. The children quickly lost interest. I have since donated the chart to an upper-grade classroom where the content is age appropriate. I altered the song to match the level and interest of the class, and the chart continues to be popular and well used.

All the interactive charts in this book have been child-tested. They have maintained their popularity and effectiveness in many classrooms. Interactive charts are powerful and enjoyable learning materials that strengthen any whole language environment. Vicki and I hope that our examples will add an enjoyable and enriching component to your classroom. Enjoy!

Kristin Schlosser

Introduction

What materials contribute to an environment that effectively guides and promotes successful reading strategies for children? Recent research in the areas of reading and language development have lent support for such materials as Big Books, predictable books, and process writing journals as key components in an environment where children are actively involved in language learning. Another addition to this list of successful materials is the interactive chart.

An interactive chart presents a poem, song, or fingerplay that provides children with an opportunity to manipulate print in a concrete way. Children are active, concrete learners who need maximum support for emergent reading behavior. They can use interactive charts to match their developing language abilities with an awareness of the way that language is represented in print.

An interactive chart uses rhythm and rhyme to support memory retention. The memorable quality enables the children to interact confidently with the text and also provides a self-checking component. As children gain control of the words, they develop a trust in print and feel secure with their abilities as emergent readers.

Interactive charts can be a powerful learning tool in affective domain development. As children manipulate the print, they are making choices and assuming ownership and responsibility for the reading process. Variables such as motivation, improved self-confidence, and autonomy develop as children experience success with print. The charts are naturally multileveled because children work at their personal comfort level. As they experience success, the level becomes increasingly more challenging. These successful experiences allow children to gain confidence in their ability to read. They begin to associate reading with pleasure and view themselves as successful readers.

This book is a compilation of interactive charts that have been used successfully for encouraging and developing beginning reading behaviors. The following categories are included: name charts, seasonal charts, number charts, functional print charts, thematic charts, and charts related to literature.

The entry for each chart includes the text for the chart, its interactive component, and additional suggestions. Many entries include reproducible components for ease in construction and personal charts for children to make and take home.

INTERACTIVE CHARTS

Questions and Answers

Why Should I Use Interactive Charts in My Classroom?

The very nature of charts appeals to children. Interactive charts are concise, attractive, and easily accessible, and they contain a rich, memorable text. As children interact and "play" with the language and print, their efforts and experimentations are rewarded.

When charts are introduced effectively and used as an integral part of a literacy program, children will replicate the reading model presented by the teacher. Children will also internalize those reading behaviors and self-practice their own developing reading strategies. The rhythmical language and repetitive structure of the charts encourage children to participate and interact with the print and provide support as the children's literacy knowledge grows through engagement with interactive charts.

Charts are an important part of the rich literate environment that children need to be immersed in within the school setting. Some advantages that charts can provide are the following:

- Charts allow children to engage in meaningful literacy activities using the natural approach they have automatically experienced through oral language development.

- Charts provide opportunities for all students to participate at varying developmental stages of reading, and they provide all students with success in a noncompetitive environment.

- Charts foster the development of literacy through social interaction with teachers and peers within the context of a community of learners.

- Charts provide an excellent means of assessing children's literacy development. Through observation, the teacher can assess the child's understanding of the conventions of print.

How Do I Make an Interactive Chart?

1. Write a poem, song, or fingerplay on sentence strips, one sentence per strip. Make sure that print is neat and consistent in size and formation, that spacing between words is adequate, and that punctuation is clear.

2. Using rubber cement or a glue stick, attach the sentence strips to a piece of poster board. A poster board that measures 24"x 36" is appropriate for displaying and storing.

3. Choose some element that the children can manipulate—rhyming words, number words, names of their classmates—in order to increase their interest in the chart. The children can match the manipulable element to the text of the chart or use it to fill in a blank space in the text.

4. Laminate the chart for durability. Attach an envelope to the back of the chart for storage of manipulable parts. Attach the envelope before laminating and cut it open with a craft knife.

What Part of the Text Should Be Manipulable?

The manipulable component of the chart should be a meaningful element of the text and dependent on the ability of the children and the objective of the chart. Choose between sentence strips for sentences or longer phrases and cards for individual words, numerals, or letters.

- **DUPLICATED SENTENCES:** Place a paper fastener or small piece of magnetic tape at the beginning and end of each sentence on the chart. Punch holes in or attach pieces of magnetic tape to the duplicated sentences that the children then match to the chart.

- **KEY WORDS, RHYMING WORDS, INITIAL WORDS, OR END WORDS:** Consider the goal of the chart when choosing which part to manipulate.

- **NUMBER WORDS:** Write the numeral or the corresponding number of dots on the back of the number word card so that children can self-check their choices.

- **CHILDREN'S NAMES:** Charts whose manipulable parts are names are always very popular.

How Do I Attach the Manipulable Component to the Chart?

Paper fasteners, magnetic tape, and self-sticking Velcro have been successful. When using paper fasteners, tape over the opened prongs on the back of the chart to keep the fasteners in place after repeated use. Attach clear pockets made of remnants of laminating material to the charts using clear book tape on the sides and bottom.

Should I Provide a Picture Cue on the Chart?

Absolutely! Pictures add to the meaning of the text and enhance the chart aesthetically. Children are drawn to visually attractive materials and often use them more frequently than other materials. Photographs are the best choice because they add a realistic quality to the chart that the children can relate to. Use photographs from magazines, posters, greeting cards, and so on.

Where Do I Find Poems, Songs, and Fingerplays for the Charts?

Children's song books, nursery rhyme books, fingerplay books, and poetry collections are all good sources for chart texts. See page 80 for a brief list of recommended sources. Check your local library, children's bookstore, music store, and next education conference. Ask colleagues for poetry and songs that they have used successfully.

What Should I Consider When Choosing the Text for a Chart?

Consider its length, child appeal, and manipulable choices.

- **LENGTH:** The length should be appropriate to the age of the children. For example, four-line poems are successful for emergent readers.

- **CHILD APPEAL:** The text should have rhyme, rhythm, and repetition so that children can easily remember and follow it. Look for a predictable text that is written in natural language. The best indicator of a good choice is whether the children use the chart repeatedly.

- **MANIPULABLE CHOICES:** Some texts immediately suggest a manipulative component. In the song "Happy Birthday," for instance, the child's name is the meaningful interactive element of the text. Read poems, songs, and fingerplays with an interactive viewpoint in mind, and feel free to change a traditional text in order to include an interactive element. For example, a traditional poem:

> The sun will shine.
> The rain will fall.
> And spring flowers
> Will grow up tall.

An interactive poem with a manipulable element:

> The sun will shine.
> The rain will fall.
> And _____ flowers
> Will grow up tall.

The children can place color words or flower names in the blank space.

How Do I Display Interactive Charts in the Classroom?

Display the charts at an appropriate height for the children. Store the manipulable parts nearby, in a box or basket under the chart, for example.

Display charts using the following:

- easel
- pegboard
- magnetic clips to attach the chart to a chalkboard
- chart stand
- low bulletin board

Store charts using the following:

- Clip parts to pants hangers and hang them on chart stands or hooks.
- Place an over-the-door clothes hanger in a closet. Clip charts to the hangers.
- Stand charts upright in a box that is large enough to hold them without bending.
- Store charts in a large artist's portfolio.

How Do I Introduce an Interactive Chart?

Modeling and demonstration are extremely important.

1. Discuss the picture cue with the children. Ask them to predict what they think the text will be about and how the picture supports this prediction.

2. Read, chant, or sing the text with enthusiasm. Point to each word with a pointer as you read and model the interactive component. This procedure enables the children to observe voice-print pairing, left-to-right progression, and other conventions of print as well as the process of manipulating the interactive component.

3. Go over the text again, this time encouraging the class to participate. The text of most of the charts can be sung, either to traditional tunes, borrowed melodies, or made-up chants. This stage of high energy and mutual enjoyment can be enhanced by singing.

4. Reread the text often in order to familiarize the children with the chart. Allow the children to dramatize the poem or song if it is appropriate.

How Often Should I Introduce an Interactive Chart?

Introduce one new chart per session and limit the number of charts according to the interests and abilities of the children. The goal—to increase familiarity and confidence—is achieved through many interactions with the same chart. Allow plenty of time for children to interact with the charts independently or in small groups. This activity gives you time to observe individual reading progress and plan for future instruction.

How Can I Increase the Children's Interactions with Charts?

- Assign personal charts as a class project. The chart can be a reproduced version of the class interactive chart for children to create independently. This book contains some reproducible personal charts.

- Provide a supply of pointers throughout the classroom. The children will use them to imitate and model the teacher, thus increasing their attraction to charts.

- Provide a supply of paper fasteners, blank index cards, pencils, and pictures for children to create their own manipulables during their free time.

- Provide time and opportunities for children to engage, interact, and explore the print on the chart.

How Can I Teach Strategies and Skills Using Interactive Charts?

Reading is taught most effectively within the context of a meaningful whole, allowing children to employ a variety of reading strategies and to construct concepts about the conventions of print. Charts provide an excellent means for children to construct relationships between oral and written language and develop important reading concepts. By effectively guiding children in focusing on the print, teachers can assist children in integrating semantic, syntactic, and grapho-phonic cuing systems.

Suggestions for strategies to focus on include the following:

- Directionality: left to right, top to bottom
- Differences between a letter, word, and sentence
- Spacing
- Punctuation
- Letter recognition
- Consonants and/or vowels
- Sound-symbol relationships: beginning sounds, ending sounds, blends, etc.
- Vocabulary and word recognition
- Rhyming words
- Compound words, root words, contractions

Procedures for Skill Focus:

- Allow the children to have repeated exposure to and experience with the text to successfully internalize its language pattern, structure, and meaning.

- Choose a skill that is appropriate for the child and/or grade level objective. Skill-focus opportunities are often student-initiated and the teacher should take advantage of these "teachable moments."

- Model and demonstrate the objective, such as circling all the words that begin with B.

- Instruct the children to complete the task.

Techniques to help the children focus on particular details of print:

- Using the cloze procedure, the teacher covers the desired focus component and allows the children to provide it. (Sticky note pads work well for this.)

- In masking, the teacher uses a cardboard frame and outlines a particular print detail.

- Children use wipe-off markers on laminated charts to circle a particular print concept.

NAME CHARTS

One of the most successful ways to engage young children in literacy learning is to focus on their names. Charts provide a variety of meaningful opportunities to incorporate the children's names. Name charts are popular and motivational and provide an excellent way for even the youngest children to validate themselves as readers.

Name Song

If your name begins
with the letter _____
hang it up right here.

INTERACTIVE COMPONENT

● Create individual upper-case letter cards for the blank space in the text.

● Create a name card for each child in the class. Children can attach their card to the chart when the letter matches the first letter in their name.

ADDITIONAL SUGGESTIONS

● You can use this chart for taking attendance or making the transition to another activity such as recess, lunch, or library.

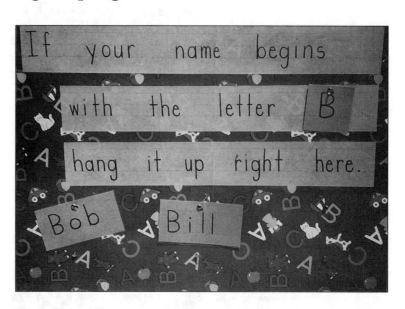

Friends

I have a friend
Whose name is _____
And we have fun together.
We laugh and play
And sing all day
In any kind of weather.

INTERACTIVE COMPONENT

● Create a name card for each child in the class to fill in the blank space in the text.

ADDITIONAL SUGGESTIONS

● You can attach a photograph of the child to the chart to correspond with the name.

Happy Birthday

Happy birthday to you,
Happy birthday to you,
Happy birthday, dear _____,
Happy birthday to you.

INTERACTIVE COMPONENT
- Create a name card for each child
  in the class to fill in the blank space in the song.
- Create candles that can be attached to the chart to reflect the child's age.

ADDITIONAL SUGGESTIONS
- Create the chart in the shape of a birthday cake to add visual appeal.
- Store the manipulable candles in a box that is wrapped to resemble a birthday present.
- Write the children's names on construction paper cutouts shaped like cakes to give as birthday mementos.

Little Red Box

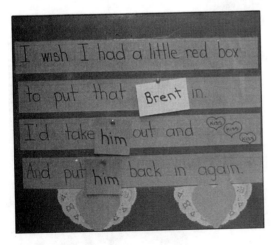

I wish I had a little red box
to put that _____ in.
I'd take _____ out and kiss kiss kiss
And put _____ back in again.

INTERACTIVE COMPONENT
- Create an individual name card for each class member for the first blank in the song.
- Create two sets of cards for the remaining spaces: two cards labeled *him* and two cards labeled *her*.

ADDITIONAL SUGGESTIONS
- The children enjoy making a smacking sound instead of singing or saying the words *kiss kiss kiss*.
- You can store the name cards in a red box placed in front of the chart. A heart-shaped candy box works well for this purpose.
- Color-code the words *him* and *her* by writing each set on a different color paper. This strategy helps emerging readers discriminate between the two words.

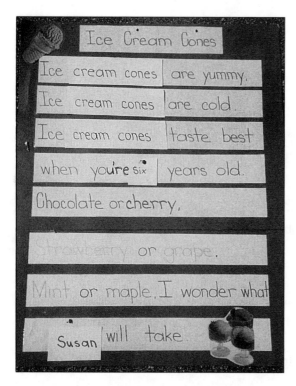

Ice Cream Cones

Ice cream cones are yummy,
Ice cream cones are cold,
Ice cream cones taste best
when you're _____ years old.
Chocolate or cherry,
Strawberry or grape,
Mint or maple, I wonder what
_____ will take.

INTERACTIVE COMPONENT

- Create number cards to reflect the ages of the children in the class for the blank space in line 4.
- Create individual name cards to fill in the blank in the last line of the chart.

ADDITIONAL SUGGESTIONS

- Decorate the chart with pictures from ice cream cone packages.
- Write the name of each flavor of ice cream in a corresponding color. For example, write *chocolate* with a brown marker.

"Ice Cream Cones" by Mary Voell Jones. Reprinted from *First Songs: The Young Child Sings*, by Mary Voell Jones. Copyright © 1976 by Mary Voell Jones. Used by permission of Paulist Press.

Shining Apples

Shining apples
Round and bright,
You are such a Fall delight!

INTERACTIVE COMPONENT

- Write each child's name on an apple shape on the chart. Provide a second personalized apple so the children can match the names.

ADDITIONAL SUGGESTIONS

- You can reproduce the text of the poem on another set of sentence strips so the children can match and sequence the text.
- You can alter this chart by attaching a picture of each child to the individual apples.
- You can use this chart as an attendance chart.

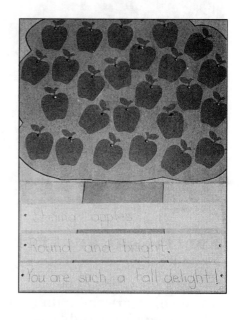

Love Somebody

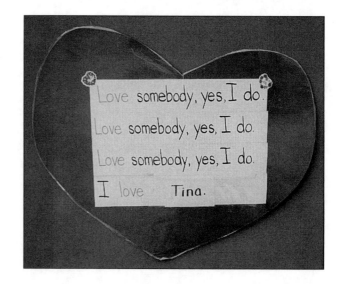

Love somebody, yes, I do.
Love somebody, yes, I do.
Love somebody, yes, I do.
I love _____.

(To the tune of "Skip to My Lou")

INTERACTIVE COMPONENT

● Create a set of name cards to fill in the blank space.

ADDITIONAL SUGGESTIONS

● Provide blank cards so that the children can write the names of family members and friends.

Look Who's Here

Look who's here.
It's _____.
They are all in school today!

INTERACTIVE COMPONENT

● Create a name card for each child in the class to hang on the chart.

ADDITIONAL SUGGESTIONS

● This chart is an excellent aid in taking attendance. Children can first observe the process and later learn to recognize names.

● Write children's names on shaped paper to add visual appeal. Change the shapes to match the season and/or theme of the classroom.

Razzle Dazzle

_____ name is _____
_____ like the sun.
_____ razzle dazzle
has just begun.
Razzle Dazzle
Sparkle and shine
Razzle Dazzle
Sparkle and shine

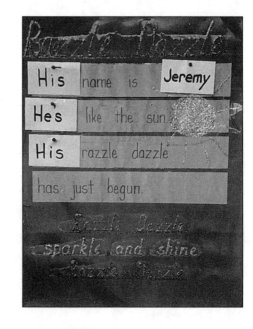

INTERACTIVE COMPONENT

* Create a set of name cards for the blank space at the end of the first line.
* Create the following pairs of word cards: *Her, She's, Her,* and *His, He's, His.* Children fill in the blanks at the beginning of the first three lines.

ADDITIONAL SUGGESTIONS

* You can use this chart to highlight a birthday or other special event.

I Am Special

My name is _____.
I have _____ at my house.
My favorite food is_____.
I want to be _____.

INTERACTIVE COMPONENT

* Create or have the children create name cards and cards with the kind of pet (*one dog, two cats,* for example), names of foods, and career words.

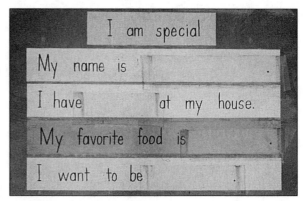

ADDITIONAL SUGGESTIONS

* Color-code each sentence and its interactive component cards. For example, write the first sentence on yellow paper and use yellow paper for all the name cards.

* You might like to prepare individual charts for the children to create and take home. Provide sentence strips that the children can glue onto construction paper in the correct order. They can illustrate their charts and create cards, using masking tape to keep them in place.

Who Stole the Cookies?

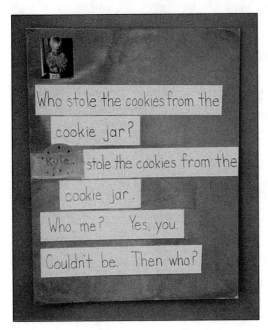

Who stole the cookies
from the cookie jar?
_____ stole the cookies
from the cookie jar.
Who, me? Yes, you.
Couldn't be.
Then who?

INTERACTIVE COMPONENT

* Create a set of name cards that the children can insert in the blank space.

ADDITIONAL SUGGESTIONS

* Write the children's names on construction paper "cookies" and keep them in a plastic cookie jar.

Patty-cake

Patty-cake, patty-cake, baker's man;
Bake me a cake as fast as you can.
Pat it and prick it, and mark
it with a _____
and put it in the oven
for _____ and me.

INTERACTIVE COMPONENT

* Create a set of upper-case letter cards to fill in the first blank space.
* Create a set of name cards for the blank space in the last line.

ADDITIONAL SUGGESTIONS

* You can use this interactive rhyme to introduce a baking activity. The children can make muffins, cookies, or cupcakes and decorate them with their initial.

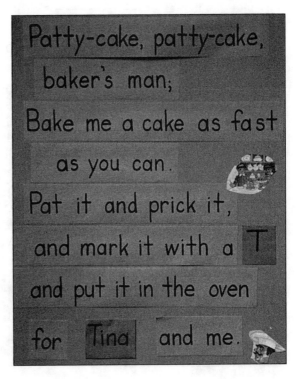

21

I Like You

I like you.
You like me.
So good friends we will be.
_____ likes _____.
_____ likes _____.
So good friends they will be.

INTERACTIVE COMPONENT

- Create a set of name cards to fill in the four blank spaces.

ADDITIONAL SUGGESTIONS

- Add pictures of the children to the name cards to aid independent use.
- Provide blank cards so children can write the names of friends or family members.

"I Like You" by Mary Voell Jones. Reprinted from *First Songs: The Young Child Sings*, by Mary Voell Jones. Copyright © 1976 by Mary Voell Jones. Used by permission of Paulist Press.

Jack Be Nimble

_____ be nimble,
_____ be quick,
_____ jump over the candlestick.

INTERACTIVE COMPONENT

- Create three sets of name cards to fill in the blank spaces.

ADDITIONAL SUGGESTIONS

- Provide a cardboard-cutout candlestick or a short stack of blocks so the children can dramatize the rhyme.
- Many familiar nursery rhymes can be made into successful interactive name charts by using your children's names in place of the character or to fill a blank space in the rhyme.

SEASONAL CHARTS

Children are interested in and delighted by seasonal themes. A wide variety of literacy resources—including seasonal songs, poems, and fingerplays—lend themselves to interactive charts. These charts provide wonderful opportunities to connect language to learning in several curriculum areas.

Leaves Falling Down

_____ leaves falling down,
_____ leaves falling down,
Over all the town,
Over all the town.

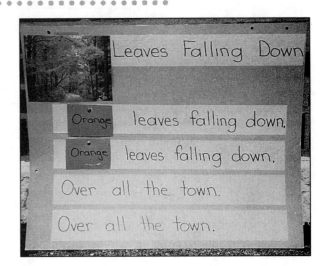

INTERACTIVE COMPONENT

- Provide pairs of color words for the blank spaces in the poem. Choose color words that match fall leaves.

ADDITIONAL SUGGESTIONS

- Write the color words on colored paper that matches the word. For example, write the word *red* on red paper.
- After the children are familiar with this chart, include it in a fall center for individual use. It adds a literate component to a traditional fall display.

Down, Down

Down, down, yellow and brown.
Leaves are falling
all over the town.

INTERACTIVE COMPONENT

- Create word cards for the children to match to the words on the chart.

ADDITIONAL SUGGESTIONS

- Write the words on construction paper cut into the shape of leaves.

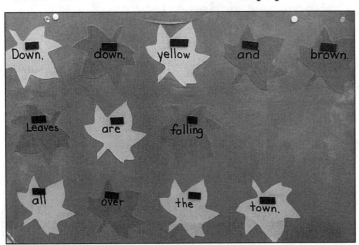

- Use different color leaves and match the words *yellow* and *brown* with the appropriate color paper.
- You might like to duplicate the poem, then have the children cut out the strips and glue them in proper sequence onto construction paper. Children can decorate the charts with leaf prints before taking them home.

The Orchard

The orchard has so many trees,
More than I've ever seen.
They are full of apples,
Red, yellow and green.

INTERACTIVE COMPONENT

* Create word cards for the children to match to the color words in the chart.

ADDITIONAL SUGGESTIONS

* Write each color word in the corresponding color. For example, write the word *red* with a red marker.
* Attach a red, yellow, or green apple shape to the corresponding word card to provide a cue.

Hibernation

Where do the _____ go when leaves turn red?
They crawl in the _____ and go to bed.
They hibernate, they hibernate,
And they don't come out till Spring.

INTERACTIVE COMPONENT

* Create pairs of word cards for the blank spaces in the chart. For example, *turtles/pond, bears/cave, foxes/den.*

ADDITIONAL SUGGESTIONS

* It is helpful for emerging readers if the word pairs are color coded. For example, write the words *turtles* and *pond* on the same color paper.
* As the children study hibernation during a fall unit, they can add new pairs to the chart. Provide blank cards and a pencil for this activity.
* You can provide a picture cue on the back of each word card to aid in independent use.

Halloween

I know there are no _____
That go flying through the air,
But I pretend on Halloween
That they are really there.

INTERACTIVE COMPONENT

● Create word cards of Halloween
characters for the blank space in the
chart: *ghosts, witches, monsters, vampires,* and so on.

ADDITIONAL SUGGESTIONS

● Use Halloween stickers for picture cues on the back of the word cards.

● Provide extra word cards or self-sticking memo paper so the children can
create new characters.

● Black poster board, orange sentence strips, and seasonal decorations make
this chart visually appealing.

"Halloween," reprinted from "Witches," by Richard C. Berg from *Music for Young Americans*, copyright © 1963,
American Book Company. Used by permission of D. C. Heath and Company.

Thanksgiving Day

The _____ ran away
Before Thanksgiving Day.
He said, "They'll make a _____ of me
If I decide to stay."

(To the tune of "The Farmer in the Dell")

INTERACTIVE COMPONENT

● Create pairs of word cards to fill in the blanks
in the song: *turkey/roast, pumpkin/pie,
cranberry/sauce, bread/stuffing.*

ADDITIONAL SUGGESTIONS

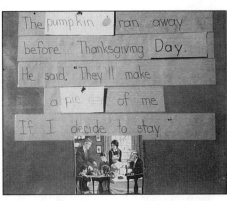

● It is helpful to color-code the word cards by
writing each pair on a different color paper.

● You may want to provide picture cues for emerging readers.

● Provide blank word cards so children can create new pairs for the song.

● This is a successful personal chart that children will enjoy making and taking
home. Have children illustrate each Thanksgiving word on page 28, then cut
the words apart and use them to fill in the blanks in the song. Attach a small
piece of masking tape to each word card to hold it in place.

Thanksgiving Day

The _____ ran away

Before Thanksgiving Day.

He said, "They'll make

a _____ of me

If I decide to stay."

Children draw a tiny picture to illustrate each of the word cards below and cut them out. Fold this paper up on the dotted line.
Staple the sides to create a pocket. Store word cards in the pocket.

turkey	roast	cranberry
sauce	pumpkin	pie

Santa

Here is the chimney.
Here is the top.
Open the lid,
Out Santa pops!

INTERACTIVE COMPONENT

* Reproduce the poem on an additional set of sentence strips. The children match the sentences to the chart.

ADDITIONAL SUGGESTIONS

* Children enjoy the movement aspect of this poem. Allow them to brainstorm motions to accompany each line.
* Because the text is so short, this poem is ideal for use in focusing on specific words and/or reinforcing sequence.

Christmas Poem

Here is the (wreath) that hangs on the door.
Here is the (tree) that stands on the floor.
Here is the (chimney) that Santa comes down.
Here is the (snow) that covers the town.

INTERACTIVE COMPONENT

* Place picture cues on the chart (see page 30) to represent the words *wreath, tree, chimney,* and *snow.*

* Provide separate word cards with both the word and the picture cue for the children to match to the chart.

ADDITIONAL SUGGESTIONS

* Teach this chart as a fingerplay and allow the children to create motions for each sentence.

* You may want to eliminate picture cues on the word cards, depending on the level and needs of the children.

A Chubby Little Snowman

A chubby little snowman
Had a carrot nose.
Along came a bunny,
And what do you suppose?
That hungry little bunny,
Looking for his lunch,
Ate that little snowman's nose,
Nibble, nibble, crunch.

(To the tune of "Sing a Song of Sixpence")

INTERACTIVE COMPONENT

* Make a snowman out of construction paper and attach it to the chart. Cut a hole in the snowman's nose and insert a plastic carrot.
* Create word cards that the children match to the words in the chart.

ADDITIONAL SUGGESTIONS

* Provide a small bunny puppet so the children can re-enact the poem.

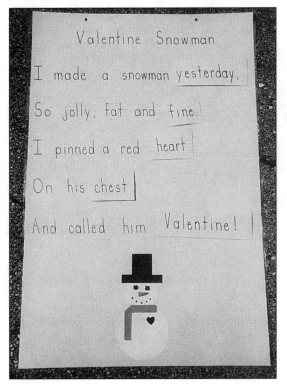

Valentine Snowman

I made a snowman yesterday,
So jolly, fat and fine.
I pinned a red heart
On his chest
And called him Valentine!

INTERACTIVE COMPONENT

* Create word cards to match the last word in each line of the text.

ADDITIONAL SUGGESTIONS

* Attach an undecorated snowman to the bottom of the chart. Provide hat, scarf, and other pieces (backed with magnetic tape) in order for the children to create a snowman. Include a heart shape to reflect the text.

31

My Valentine

My Valentine is red.
My Valentine is blue.
I drop it in the mailbox
And mail it to you.

INTERACTIVE COMPONENT

- Reproduce each line of the text on a sentence strip that the children can match to the chart. This activity reinforces sequencing in a concrete way.

ADDITIONAL SUGGESTIONS

- Shape the chart like a mailbox to add visual appeal.
- You can use this chart as a mailbox by cutting a mail slot and placing an empty box behind the chart. Encourage the children to use it to send their class valentines.

A Letter

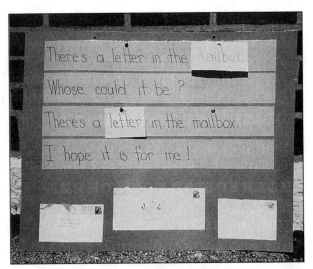

There's a letter in the mailbox.
Whose could it be?
There's a letter in the mailbox.
I hope it is for me!

INTERACTIVE COMPONENT

- Create word cards for the children to match to words in the chart.

ADDITIONAL SUGGESTIONS

- You can eliminate the final word in the poem and substitute name cards for the children in the class.
- Mount actual letters on the bottom of the chart to add visual appeal and provide a picture cue.
- You may want to use this poem to highlight vocabulary words for a Valentine or post office unit.
- Use this chart as a message board by placing an envelope with the name of a child over the final word and including a letter for him or her.

Spring Planting

Dig a little hole,
Plant a little seed.
Pour on a little water,
Pull a little weed.
Chase a little bug,
Heigh-ho, there he goes.
Give a little sunshine,
Let it grow, grow, grow.

Dig a little hole,
Plant a little seed.
Pour on a little water.
Pull a little weed.
Chase a little bug,
Heigh-ho, there he goes.
Give a little sunshine,
Let it grow, grow, grow.

INTERACTIVE COMPONENT

- Reproduce the text on sentence strips that the children can match to the chart. This activity reinforces concepts of print and sequencing in a concrete way.

ADDITIONAL SUGGESTIONS

- Allow the children to create motions for each line of the poem.
- Add a picture cue at the end of each line to help emergent readers.
- This chart is a useful literate accompaniment to traditional classroom planting of spring seeds.

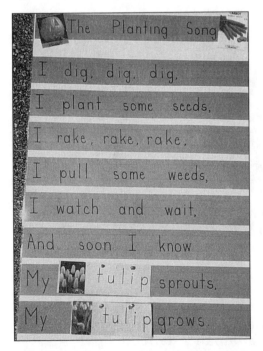

The Planting Song

I dig, dig, dig,
I plant some seeds,
I rake, rake, rake,
I pull some weeds,
I watch and wait,
And soon I know
My tulip sprouts,
My tulip grows.

The Planting Song

I dig, dig, dig,
I plant some seeds,
I rake, rake, rake,
I pull some weeds,
I watch and wait,
And soon I know
My _____ sprouts,
My _____ grows.

INTERACTIVE COMPONENT

- Create matching pairs of flower and vegetable word cards to fill in the blank spaces in the song.

ADDITIONAL SUGGESTIONS

- Attach picture cues from seed catalogs or seed packets to the word cards.

Little Seed

I'm a little seed in the ground,
Rolled up in a tiny ball.
I'll wait for rain and sunshine
To make me big and tall.

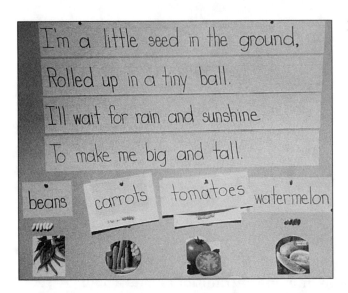

INTERACTIVE COMPONENT

* Attach word cards of familiar garden plants at the bottom of this chart. Include a picture cue and some actual seeds. Provide another set of word cards with seeds for the children to match to the words. Children can self-check their responses using the print and/or the seeds.

ADDITIONAL SUGGESTIONS

* Cut picture cues from the front of seed packets.
* Children are fascinated by the texture of the real seeds. Apply the seeds with a hot glue gun to ensure their durability. Provide a magnifying glass for further investigation.

Daffodil

A little yellow cup,
A little yellow frill,
A little yellow star,
And that's a daffodil.

INTERACTIVE COMPONENT

* Create matching sentence strips that the children can match to the chart.

ADDITIONAL SUGGESTIONS

* To make individual charts, copy the poem and have the children cut out the strips. After they glue the strips to construction paper in proper sequence, they can decorate their chart with a drawing or a paper daffodil.
* The children can make a daffodil as a craft project using a cutout paper star, cupcake paper, and green paper stem and leaves.

34

Baby Chick

Peck, Peck, Peck
on the warm brown egg.
Out comes a neck,
Out comes a leg.
How does a chick
that's not been about
discover the trick
of how to get out?

INTERACTIVE COMPONENT

* Create word cards for children to match to the chart.

ADDITIONAL SUGGESTIONS

* Create the chart in an egg shape that opens to reveal the chick inside.
* Cover the word *chick* with word cards of animals that hatch from eggs, such as *duck, frog,* and *alligator*. Create animals to accompany the new word cards. Cut pictures from nature magazines or make them from construction paper. Place the animals in the egg to match the text.

"Baby Chick" by Aileen Fisher. Copyright © Aileen Fisher. Reprinted by permission of the author.

One striped tiger
Two fat hippos
Three thick elephants
Four tall
Five lazy
in the zoo.
Would you like

NUMBER CHARTS

Many poems, songs, and fingerplays provide an excellent context for the introduction and exploration of numerical concepts. When these texts are written in interactive chart form, they provide opportunities for children to actively engage with numerical signs and symbols, patterns, and relationships. Number charts are of great interest to the children and foster both language and mathematical learning.

Ten in the Bed

There were _____
in the bed,
and the little one said,
"Roll over, roll over."
So they all rolled over
and one fell out.

INTERACTIVE COMPONENT

* As a child turns the wheel, the numeral in the text matches the number of bear stickers in the window at the top of the chart. For the numeral 1, write *was* on a self-sticking memo and tape it over the word *were*.

* To make the chart:
  1. Cut two large circles out of poster board. Attach the poem to one circle.
  2. Cut out "windows" on the circle with the poem.
  3. Fasten the circles together with a brass fastener in the middle.
  4. Attach 10 bear stickers in a semicircle to the bottom circle. They will show through the semicircular "window." Write the number 10 on the bottom circle. It will show through the square "window." Turn the bottom circle counterclockwise so that 9 stickers show in the semicircular window. Write 9 to show through the square window. Turn again to show 8 stickers and write the number 8. Continue until only 1 sticker shows and write 1.

ADDITIONAL SUGGESTIONS

* The format of this chart works successfully for any counting song, such as "Ten Green and Speckled Frogs" and "Five Little Ducks."

* Make a personal mini-chart for each child. (See page 39.)

Circle A

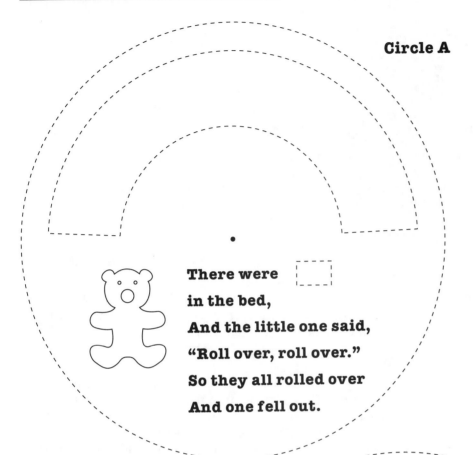

There were ☐
in the bed,
And the little one said,
"Roll over, roll over."
So they all rolled over
And one fell out.

Directions:

1. Cut out Circle A along the dashed lines, including both windows.

2. Cut out Circle B along the dashed line.

3. Place Circle A on top of Circle B. Pierce dot with a brass fastener and attach.

Circle B

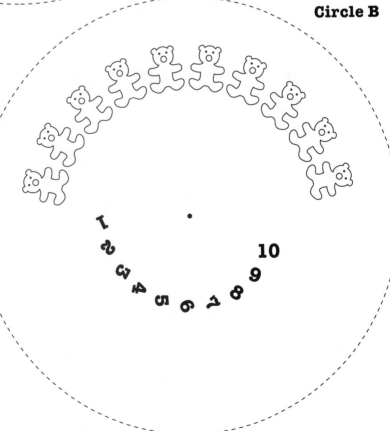

39

Bees

Here is the beehive.
Where are the bees?
Hiding away where nobody sees.
Count them as they come out of
the hive.
1-2-3-4-5. Bzzzz.

INTERACTIVE COMPONENT

* Create numerals 1 through 5 and attach them to the chart. Attach a piece of magnetic tape to each numeral.

* Make or purchase five bees and attach magnetic tape to the bottom of each one. Make a construction paper hive and attach five pieces of magnetic tape to it. Children manipulate the bees as they say the rhyme.

ADDITIONAL SUGGESTIONS

* Children might enjoy constructing and taking home an individual chart. Give children sheets of black paper on which to draw or paint a beehive on the left-hand side. On the right-hand side, children draw a random number of bees. Distribute copies of the poem that the children staple over the drawings of the bees. Have each child count the bees he or she has drawn and write the total number in the last line of the poem.

Ten Little Monkeys

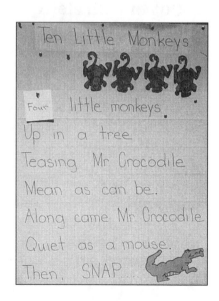

_____ little monkeys
Up in a tree
Teasing Mr. Crocodile,
Mean as can be.
Along came Mr. Crocodile,
Quiet as a mouse.
Then, SNAP. . . .

INTERACTIVE COMPONENT

* Create number cards from *ten* to *one* to use in the blank.
* Create ten monkey cutouts that can be removed to reflect the changing text.

ADDITIONAL SUGGESTIONS

* Encourage the children to create motions to dramatize the poem.
* A crocodile puppet adds appeal and allows the children to act out the poem.

Salty Pretzels

One salty pretzel,
Two salty pretzels,
Three salty pretzels,
Four.
We'll roll and roll and shape
    and bake
And then make many more!

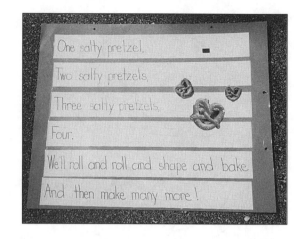

INTERACTIVE COMPONENT

* Create number cards from *one* to *four* for the children to match to the words in the chart.

ADDITIONAL SUGGESTIONS

* Attach pictures of individual pretzels that children can manipulate to illustrate the text. Cut out pictures from boxes of frozen pretzels.
* You can use this chart to introduce or extend a pretzel cooking project.

Zoo Animals

One striped tiger,
Two fat hippos,
Three thick elephants,
Four tall giraffes,
Five lazy lions
    in the zoo,
Would you like to see
    them, too?

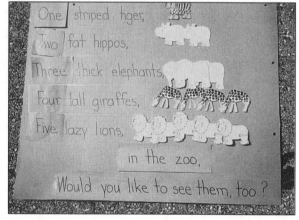

INTERACTIVE COMPONENT

* Create number cards from *one* through *five* to match to the words on the chart.
* Create animal cutouts as specified by the poem. As the children read the poem, they can manipulate the chart by matching the numbers or by attaching the specified number of animals.

ADDITIONAL SUGGESTIONS

* To make the number cards self-checking, glue the corresponding number of animals on the back of each card.

1 Little Snowman

1 little	6 little snowmen
2 little	7 little
3 little snowmen	8 little
4 little	9 little snowmen
5 little	10 little snowmen bright

(To the tune of "Ten Little Indians")

INTERACTIVE COMPONENT

● Create cards for the numerals 1 to 10 and 10 small snowmen that can be attached to the chart. Children can attach the cards and the snowmen as they sing the song.

ADDITIONAL SUGGESTIONS

● Use snowmen stickers or small plastic snowmen as the interactive component.

● Create a set of word cards for the numbers *one* through *ten* to use instead of the numeral cards.

● Children often enjoy making their own extensions of this chart. "Ten Little Indian Boys/Girls" and "Ten Cuddly Teddy Bears" are two popular variations.

Five Little Snowmen

_____ little snowmen all made of snow,
_____ little snowmen standing in a row,
Out came the sun and stayed all day
And one little snowman melted away.

INTERACTIVE COMPONENT

● Create two sets of cards with the number words *five* through *one*. Children change the cards as they say the rhyme.

● Place five detachable snowmen at the bottom of the chart. The children remove a snowman each time one "melts."

● Write the word *snowman* on two cards so the first two lines can be appropriately changed to "One little snowman. . . ."

ADDITIONAL SUGGESTIONS

● Make a finger mitt using a glove, white pom-poms, and felt. The children can re-enact the poem using the mitt.

The Apple Tree

Way up high in the apple tree
_____ little apple _____ smiled at me.
I shook that tree as hard as I could.
Down came an apple and m-m-m, was it good!

INTERACTIVE COMPONENT

- Create a set of cards for the numerals 1 to 10 that children use in the first blank. (See page 17 for reproducible apple shapes.)
- Create a card with an *s* so the children can make the word *apple* plural when appropriate.

ADDITIONAL SUGGESTIONS

- This chart provides an excellent opportunity to discuss plurals as the children decide when to add an *s* to the word *apple*.
- Children can make an individual chart by cutting an apple tree out of construction paper and stamping an apple slice dipped in paint on their tree several times. They can then count their apples and write the corresponding numeral or number word in the text that you have copied and distributed.

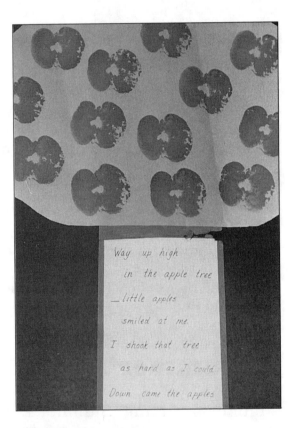

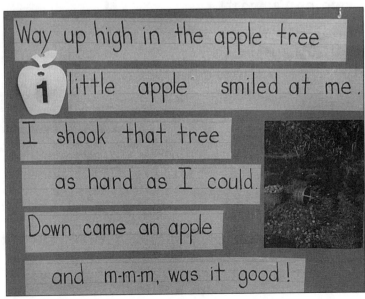

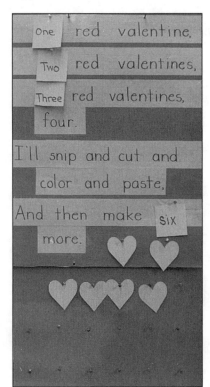

Red Valentines

One red valentine,
Two red valentines,
Three red valentines,
four.
I'll snip and cut and color and paste,
And then make _____ more.

INTERACTIVE COMPONENT

- Create a set of number cards that children match to the words *one, two, three* in the text, and use to fill in the blank space.
- Create hearts hung by paper fasteners for the bottom of the chart. Children can match the number of hearts to the text of the poem.

ADDITIONAL SUGGESTIONS

- To include a self-checking component, write the numeral and/or a set of matching dots on the reverse side of each number card.
- Write the name of each child on a heart at the bottom of the chart to add a personal touch.

Summer's Coming!

Summer's coming, Summer's coming,
We can't wait, we can't wait!
School is almost out now,
School is almost out now!
_____ more days, _____ more days!

(To the tune of "Frère Jacques")

INTERACTIVE COMPONENT

- Create two sets of identical number cards for the blank spaces in the chart. Children can manipulate them daily to indicate the number of days remaining before summer vacation.

ADDITIONAL SUGGESTIONS

- Children can make an individual copy of this chart and staple to it a paper chain with as many links as there are days remaining in the school year. They also make two sets of number cards to attach to their chart with masking tape. This then becomes a countdown instrument for use at home.

FUNCTIONAL PRINT CHARTS

Functional print charts serve a useful purpose within the structure of the classroom environment by providing natural opportunities for children to develop literacy knowledge through meaningful print. Attendance charts, job charts, cooking and craft direction charts, and daily schedule charts are among the charts that provide children with repeated encounters with print. They incorporate literacy into daily classroom routines and functional activities.

Teachers who may not yet feel confident about making or using interactive materials will find this section a helpful guide to converting familiar classroom charts to interactive charts.

Job Chart

INTERACTIVE COMPONENT

* Create name cards to place next to a picture of a classroom area to indicate children's jobs during cleanup time. Change names on a daily or weekly schedule.

ADDITIONAL SUGGESTIONS

* Use actual photographs of classroom areas to add clarity.

* You may want to occasionally post a job request chart where the children can sign up for a desired job. This chart encourages the use of functional print and adds an element of choice to classroom jobs.

* After they have completed the assigned job, the children may post a *closed* sign to signal that the area has been cleaned and is therefore no longer available for activities. The *closed* signs are another way to add purposeful, functional print to the classroom environment.

Snack Chart

Today's snack is _____.
Today's drink is _____.

INTERACTIVE COMPONENT

* Create word cards for snack and drink items to fill in the blank spaces. Change the chart to reflect daily snack choices.

ADDITIONAL SUGGESTIONS

* You may want to add picture cues to the word cards to help emergent readers.

Work Completion Chart

INTERACTIVE COMPONENT

* Children write their name on a strip of paper and place it in a personalized library pocket, signaling that they have completed their assignment.

ADDITIONAL SUGGESTIONS

* Before you write any names on this chart, laminate it and cut the pockets open with scissors or a craft knife. Write the names on the individual pockets with a permanent marker, which can be easily removed with nail polish remover. This procedure ensures the use and durability of the chart for many years.

* This chart allows children to use and view print for functional purposes. It also creates a system in which each child is responsible for the accountability of assigned projects.

* You can alter this chart for emergent readers. If the children are not yet comfortable with name writing or recognition, create a name card for each child. As the children complete their projects, they match the name card to the name on the chart and then insert the card in the pocket.

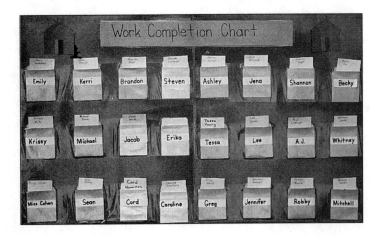

Will You Cook?

INTERACTIVE COMPONENT

* Children attach their name card in the appropriate column to indicate their desire to participate in a cooking project.

* Provide lots of space in the *yes* column because cooking is usually a popular activity.

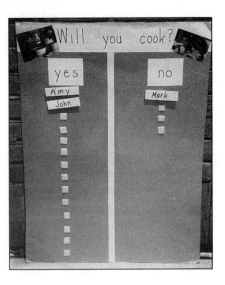

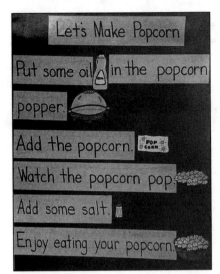

Recipe Chart

INTERACTIVE COMPONENT

● Write the steps of the recipe on the chart and create a set of identical sentence strips that the children match and sequence.

ADDITIONAL SUGGESTIONS

● Laminate the chart and additional sentence strips before writing the recipe. Write the recipe with a permanent marker that can be removed with nail polish remover. This allows you to use the chart for every cooking experience.

● The children can use the chart independently during free time to sequence the recipe steps.

● You may want to reproduce the recipe and cut apart the steps. Children glue the steps to construction paper in correct order to take home.

Attendance Chart

INTERACTIVE COMPONENT

● Create the chart and a set of name cards. Children place their name card in their pocket when they enter the classroom.

● Cut 3"x 22" strips of oak tag. Place the strips 4" apart on a large piece of oak tag that measures 22" x 36". Use colored plastic tape to tape the bottom of each strip. Place vertical strips of tape 5 1/4" apart to create pockets. Laminate the entire chart. Cut the pockets open with a craft knife. Write each child's name on a pocket with a permanent marker that can be removed with nail polish remover.

ADDITIONAL SUGGESTIONS

● When children are first learning to identify their names, arrange the pockets in the same order as the rows of seats.

● You can also arrange the children's names in alphabetical order to encourage an understanding of the organizational system of the alphabet.

● Change the shape of the name cards to correlate with the seasons or units of study. (See reproducible apple shapes on page 17 and leaf shapes on page 25.)

● When children are secure with identifying their first name, add last names to the chart.

Center Time Chart

INTERACTIVE COMPONENT

* Create name cards that the children place next to a photograph of one of the classroom centers. The number of children allowed in each center is dictated by the number of spaces for names.

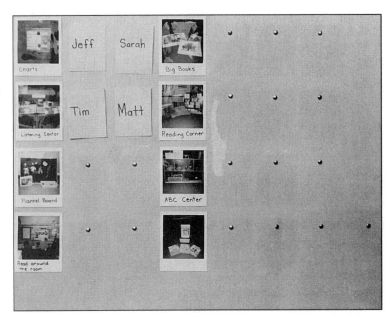

ADDITIONAL SUGGESTIONS

* This chart provides an excellent management system for center time. The children can immediately see which centers are open and which are no longer available.

* Attach a clear pocket at the bottom of the chart in which to place a sign for a special center that is not available every day. For example, "We will make pudding at the cooking table today."

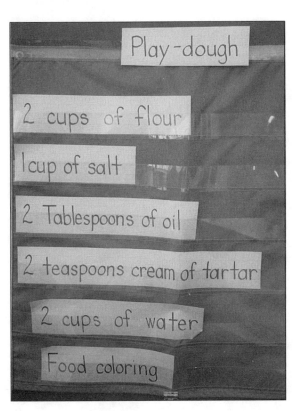

Pocket Charts

INTERACTIVE COMPONENT

* Create two sets of identical sentence strips for the recipe. Arrange one set in the pocket chart. Pass the other set of strips out to individual students as "job cards." The child whose job card matches the first strip in the chart adds that ingredient, and so on.

ADDITIONAL SUGGESTIONS

* If possible, divide the class into small groups so that each child in the group receives a job card.

* Pocket charts are an easy way to incorporate functional print into the classroom. Use them for sentence strips that give recipe ingredients or any other step-by-step process.

THEMATIC CHARTS

Thematic charts are an important aspect of a whole language classroom. Highly motivational, themes provide a meaningful context in which to connect language and integrate curriculum. Thematic charts present opportunities to incorporate the rich language of poems, songs, chants, and predictable segments of literature into a particular topic.

In the Morning

This is the way we

_____ our teeth,

_____ our teeth,

_____ our teeth.

This is the way we

_____ our teeth,

So early in the morning.

(To the tune of "Here We Go Round the Mulberry Bush")

INTERACTIVE COMPONENT

* Create four identical tooth-care word cards for the children to use in the blank spaces in the song. Some choices might include *brush*, *floss*, and *rinse*.

ADDITIONAL SUGGESTIONS

* Write each set of tooth-care words on a different color paper. For example, write the four cards for *floss* on green paper.

Colors

I can sing the colors.
You can sing them too.
Red and green and yellow,
Purple and orange and blue.

INTERACTIVE COMPONENT

* Create color word cards for the children to match to the text.

ADDITIONAL SUGGESTIONS

* Write each color word with a marker of the corresponding color. For example, write the word *red* with a red marker.

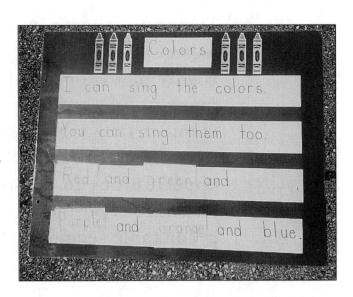

A Kite

A _____ kite is lots of fun,
So grab the string and run, run, run.
Watch it go up in the sky
Because a kite is meant to fly!

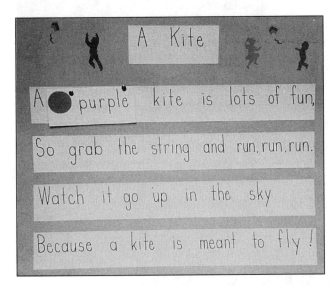

INTERACTIVE COMPONENT

- Create color word cards for the children to fill in the blank space in the text.

ADDITIONAL SUGGESTIONS

- Attach to the word card a small circle of colored paper that corresponds to the color word as a visual cue for emergent readers.

Pickles

My mother gave me a nickel
To buy a pickle.
But I didn't buy a pickle.
I bought some _____.

INTERACTIVE COMPONENT

- Create food word cards to be used in the final blank of the chart.

ADDITIONAL SUGGESTIONS

- The children love to create their own endings for this chart. Provide blank paper and pencil for their use.
- Add picture cues from cooking magazines.

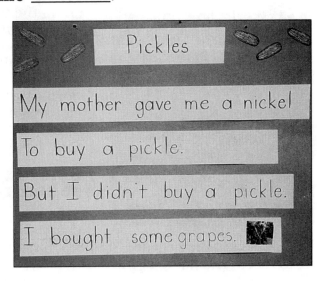

The Railroad Track

A _____ was on a railroad track,
Its heart was all a-flutter.
Along came a choo-choo train.
Toot, toot, _____.

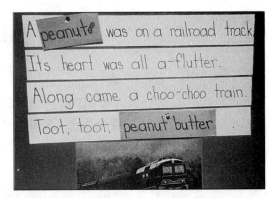

INTERACTIVE COMPONENT

• Create pairs of word cards, using food items that change form, such as *peanut/peanut butter, cracker/crumbs, tomato/catsup, grape/jelly.* Children fill in the blank spaces in the chart with the correct pair in the correct order.

ADDITIONAL SUGGESTIONS

• It is helpful if the pairs are color coded. Write each pair on matching paper. For example, write the words *peanut* and *peanut butter* on yellow paper.

• The children can create their own word pairs for this chart. Provide blank paper and pencil for independent use.

• Attach a picture cue to each word card for emerging readers.

Can You Name the Fish?

This is a _____.
This is a _____.
This is a _____.

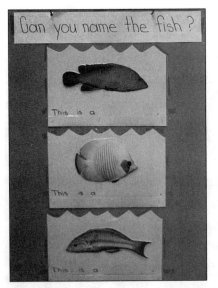

INTERACTIVE COMPONENT

• Create word cards, using the fish names that correspond to the photographs. Children match the word cards to the pictures in order to finish the sentences.

ADDITIONAL SUGGESTIONS

• You can make a chart with fish-

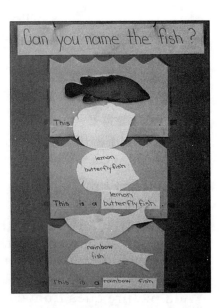

shaped greeting cards. Children can check their answers by opening the card to reveal the name of the fish.

What Animal Is in the Cage?

INTERACTIVE COMPONENT

● Create the chart by gluing zoo animal photographs to a piece of poster board. Label the animals. Create cages by cutting narrow slits in black construction paper squares so that the animals can be partially seen through the openings. Tape the tops of the "cages" over the photographs so children can lift them to reveal the animals.

● Create animal word cards that correspond to the labeled photographs on the chart. Children guess what animal is in the cage, attach the word card, and lift the cage to check their answer.

ADDITIONAL SUGGESTIONS

● Actual photographs from a class zoo trip are ideal for this chart. The children especially enjoy seeing themselves in the photos.

● Glue picture cues on the back of the word cards to aid emergent readers.

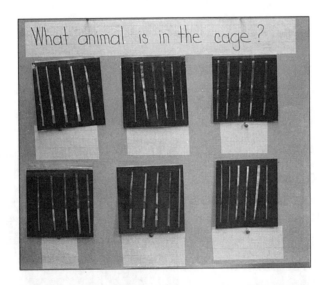

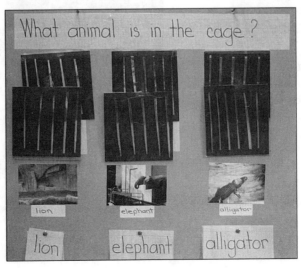

Bingo

There was a farmer
who had a dog
and Bingo was his name-o.
B-I-N-G-O
B-I-N-G-O
B-I-N-G-O
and Bingo was his name-o.

(To the traditional tune)

INTERACTIVE COMPONENT

- Create five vertical strips that the children can hang on top of the columns of letters as they sing the song. Each strip can be illustrated with three pairs of hands clapping.

ADDITIONAL SUGGESTIONS

- Sing the song through once together. The second time, place a strip over the row of B's. The children clap instead of saying *B* and sing *I-N-G-O*. Continue substituting a strip and having the children clap for each succeeding letter until you have replaced all five letters.

- Children also enjoy enacting the song with a puppet that you can make from a glove, dog pom-poms, and felt letters.

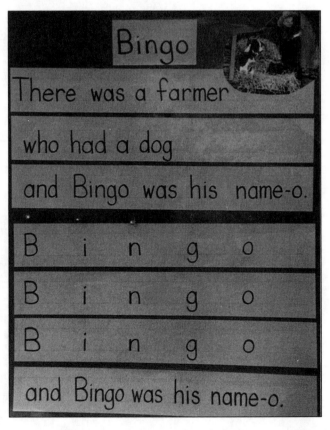

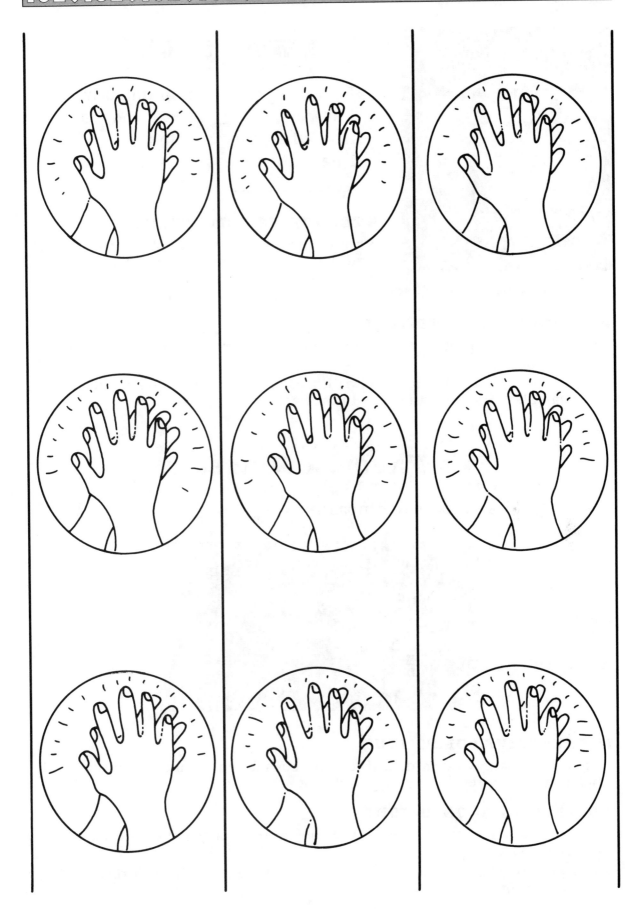

I Went to Visit

I went to visit a farm one day.
I saw a _____ across the way.
And what do you think
I heard it say?

_____

INTERACTIVE COMPONENT

● Create pairs of word cards using farm animals and the sound they make: *cow/moo, moo, moo; horse/neigh, neigh, neigh; sheep/baa, baa, baa.* Children fill in the blanks with the correct pair in the correct order.

ADDITIONAL SUGGESTIONS

● You can adapt this chart for use in other units. For example, "I went to visit a zoo one day."

● You can color-code the cards by writing each pair on matching colored paper. You can also attach picture cues to the backs of the cards.

My Favorite Dinosaur

My favorite dinosaur is _____.

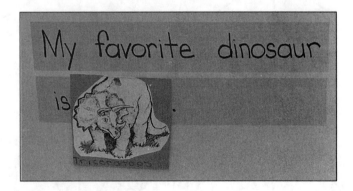

INTERACTIVE COMPONENT

● Create dinosaur word cards with picture cues for children to fill in the blank space in the sentence.

ADDITIONAL SUGGESTIONS

● Use dinosaur stickers for the picture cues or reproduce pictures from dinosaur books.

● This chart is ideal for extending literacy into the science area during a dinosaur unit.

Dinosaur

Dinosaur, dinosaur,
Tramping all around.
Dinosaur, dinosaur,
Their bones are all we found.
Dinosaur, dinosaur,
Lived so long ago.
Dinosaur fossils
Tell us all we'll ever know.

INTERACTIVE COMPONENT

● Create three pairs of word cards for *Dinosaur* and *dinosaur*. As the children match the cards to the text, they discriminate between the upper-case and lower-case initial letters.

ADDITIONAL SUGGESTIONS

● This poem is an effective chant whose rhythmic quality can be accented by using instruments.

"Dinosaur" by Betsy Frame. Copyright © Betsy Frame. Reprinted by permission of the author.

R-A-I-N-Y

There was a time
When we got wet
And RAINY was the weather.
R-A-I-N-Y
R-A-I-N-Y
R-A-I-N-Y
And RAINY was the weather.

(To the tune of "Bingo")

INTERACTIVE COMPONENT

● Create letter strips for the portion of the song where the word *rainy* is spelled out, and hang them on the chart. As the children sing the song, they remove each strip in turn, revealing a picture of clapping hands, which reminds the children to clap instead of sing. (See page 59 for a reproducible picture of clapping hands.)

ADDITIONAL SUGGESTIONS

● This chart is an excellent way to introduce, reinforce, or review isolated letter names.

Rain

Rain on the rooftops.
Rain on the trees.
Rain on the green grass.
But not on me!

INTERACTIVE COMPONENT

● Create word cards for *rooftops, trees, grass,* and *me.* As the children match the cards to the chart, they focus on last words in a concrete way.

ADDITIONAL SUGGESTIONS

● Place a picture cue on the back of each word card to aid emerging readers.

● You can adapt the text of this chart to make individual books for each child. Reproduce one line per page and allow the children to illustrate each page. The children can refer to the chart for assistance in decoding and sequencing the book pages.

Fire Fighters

Fire fighters wear big red _____,
Climb up _____ to rescue _____,
Use big _____ to spray on _____,
Ride big _____ with big black _____,
Race when they hear a _____ alarm,
To help keep _____ safe from harm.

INTERACTIVE COMPONENT

● Create pictures to fill in the blanks in the chart.

● Create word cards for the words *hats, ladders, cats, hoses, fires, trucks, tires, fire, people.* The children place the word card over the appropriate picture on the chart.

ADDITIONAL SUGGESTIONS

● You may want to provide visual clues on the back of the word cards.

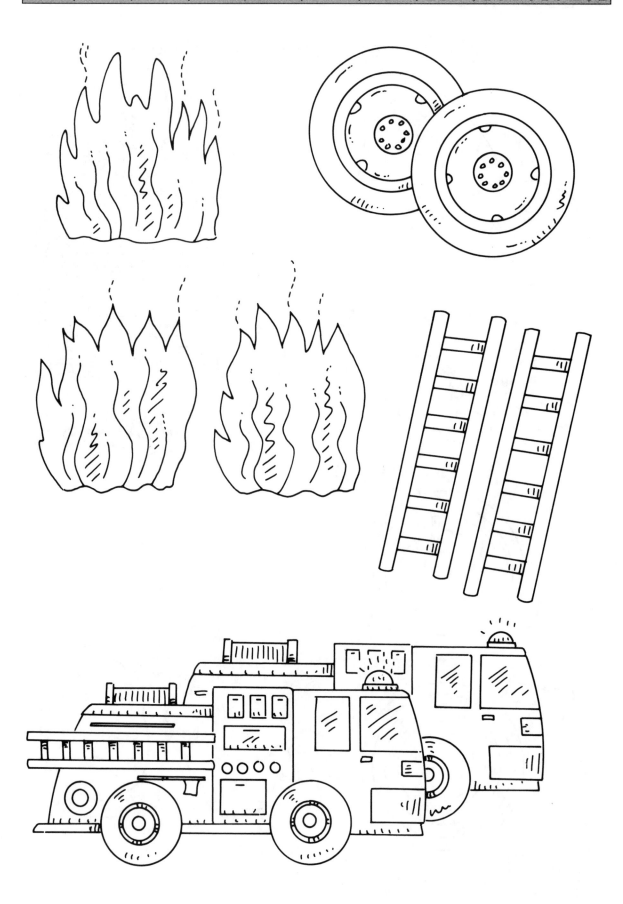

The Eensy-Weensy Spider

The eensy-weensy spider
Climbed up the waterspout.
Down came the rain
And washed the spider out.
Out came the sun
And dried up all the rain.
And the eensy-weensy spider
Climbed up the spout again.

INTERACTIVE COMPONENT

● Create word cards that the children match to words in the chart.

ADDITIONAL SUGGESTIONS

● Create a cloud, a sun, and a pom-pom spider that the children can manipulate as they read the poem.
● The children can add hand motions and sing the text.

The Caterpillars

"Let's go to sleep," the caterpillars said,
As they tucked themselves into bed.
They will awaken by and by,
And each will be a lovely butterfly!

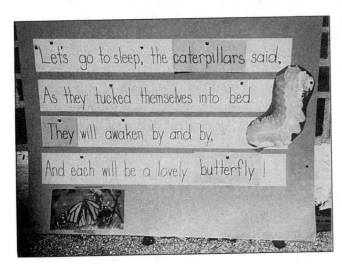

INTERACTIVE COMPONENT

● Create word cards for the children to match to words in the text. You may want to emphasize vocabulary for a unit on spring or insects.

ADDITIONAL SUGGESTIONS

● Allow the children to create motions to accompany each line of the poem.

Butterfly

Brightly colored butterfly
Looking for honey,
Spread your wings and fly away
While it's sunny.

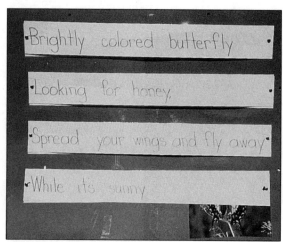

INTERACTIVE COMPONENT

- Reproduce the text on sentence strips that the children match to the chart, reinforcing visual perception skills, concepts of print, and sequencing.

ADDITIONAL SUGGESTIONS

- Allow the children to brainstorm motions for each line of the poem so they can act it out.

Teddy Bear

Teddy bear, Teddy bear, turn around.
Teddy bear, Teddy bear, touch the ground.
Teddy bear, Teddy bear, climb the stairs.
Teddy bear, Teddy bear, say your prayers.

INTERACTIVE COMPONENT

- Create word cards for the children to match to words in the poem. The words *Teddy bear* are ideal for this task because they are repeated so often throughout the poem.

ADDITIONAL SUGGESTIONS

- Write the action component of each sentence on a sentence strip that the children can match to the text as they dramatize the poem. Glue a picture cue for the action on the back of each card.

- After the children are familiar with the poem, you can alter it to create a new poem. Cover the action components with blank sentence strips and allow the children to brainstorm new phrases. This activity allows the children to experience semantics and rhyme in a concrete way.

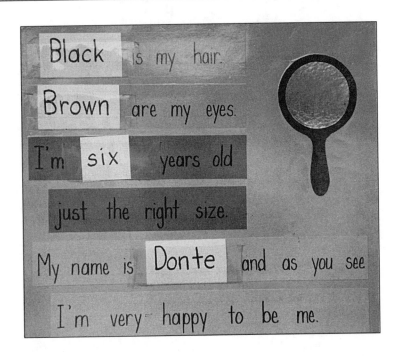

I'm Very Happy to Be Me

_____ is my hair.

_____ are my eyes.

I'm _____ years old

just the right size.

My name is _____ and as you see

I'm very happy to be me.

INTERACTIVE COMPONENT

● Create a set of name cards and three sets of word cards for the blank spaces in the chart:

  1. Blonde/Red/Brown/Black

  2. Blue/Green/Brown

  3. five/six/seven

  As the children chant the rhyme, they fill in the blanks with the appropriate cards.

ADDITIONAL SUGGESTIONS

● Color-code the sentences and corresponding word cards to aid the children in independent use.

● Attach a mirror made from construction paper and Mylar to add visual appeal to the chart.

● This rhyme makes an excellent individual chart. The children complete each line with the appropriate information and add a self-portrait.

In the dark, dark box
there was a _____

Shoe

CHARTS RELATED
TO LITERATURE

Varied and rich interactions with literature expose children to many forms
of language and literacy. Children are
highly motivated to involve themselves
with charts that relate to their favorite
books. Interactive charts allow children to extend literature in a meaningful and concrete way.

Clouds

I thought I saw a _____
way up in the sky.
I thought I saw so many things
as clouds went drifting by.

INTERACTIVE COMPONENT

* Create word cards that children can fill in the blank space in the poem. Suggestions include a pig, a horse, and an ice cream cone.

ADDITIONAL SUGGESTIONS

* You can correlate this chart with the book *It Looked Like Spilt Milk* by Charles G. Shaw or *Dreams* by Peter Spier. Refer to these books for additional cloud shape suggestions.

* Use blue poster board and white sentence strips to add visual appeal to this chart.

* Allow the children to observe clouds and create new word cards for the chart. Provide blank cards for the activity.

* This chart is an ideal personal chart. Each child can create a word card to fill in the blank and illustrate the chart with cotton balls.

"Clouds" by Sally Moomaw. From *Discovering Music in Early Childhood* by Sally Moomaw, copyright © 1984. Reprinted by permission of the author.

Here We Go

Here we go to the beach,
to the beach,
to the beach.
Here we go to the beach.
We can pack _____.

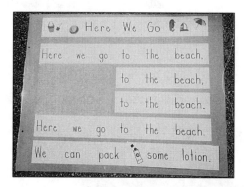

(To the tune of "Here We Go Round the Mulberry Bush")

INTERACTIVE COMPONENT

* Create word cards with picture cues that children fill in the blank space in the chart. Suggested items for the cards include a shovel, a float, and a swimsuit.

ADDITIONAL SUGGESTIONS

* Allow the children to brainstorm the beach items for the cards.

* You can correlate this chart with *At the Beach* by Anne Rockwell. Refer to the book for additional items for the word cards.

The Gingerbread Man

Run, run, as fast as you can.
You can't catch me,
I'm the Gingerbread Man.
I ran away from
_____.

INTERACTIVE COMPONENT

* Create a set of word cards using the names of the characters in your favorite version of *The Gingerbread Man*. The children use the cards to complete the text.

ADDITIONAL SUGGESTIONS

* This chart makes an excellent individual chart. The children can cut out strips with the names of the story characters and sequence them according to the story.

Planting a Rainbow

Mom and _____ plant a rainbow.
It will soon be spring, you know.
They will plant _____ seeds
And watch the rainbow grow!

INTERACTIVE COMPONENT

* Create a name card for each child in the class for the first blank space in the poem.
* Create flower word cards for the second blank space.

ADDITIONAL SUGGESTIONS

* You can correlate this chart with *Planting a Rainbow* by Lois Ehlert. Refer to the book for suggestions for the flower names.

* Use actual seed packets instead of word cards in the second blank space of the poem.

Mary, Mary

Mary, Mary, quite contrary,
How does your garden grow?
With _____ and _____
And pretty maids all in a row.

INTERACTIVE COMPONENT

* Create two sets of cards using the names of different flowers for the children to fill in the blank spaces.

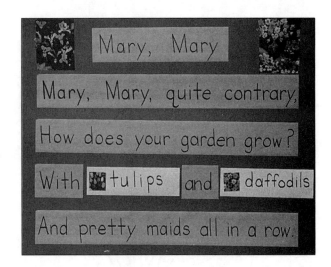

ADDITIONAL SUGGESTIONS

* You can correlate this chart with the book *Tomie dePaola's Mother Goose.* Many other familiar Mother Goose rhymes also lend themselves to interactive charts.
* Provide a picture cue on each word card from flower and seed catalogs.
* Children enjoy making their own individual charts from this rhyme.

There Was an Old Lady Who Swallowed a Fly

There was an old lady who
swallowed a _____.

INTERACTIVE COMPONENT

* Create animal word cards with pictures cues for the children to fill in the blank space in the text.

ADDITIONAL SUGGESTIONS

* You can correlate this chart with *I Know an Old Lady Who Swallowed a Fly* by Nadine Bernard Westcott. Refer to the book for the sequence of the animals.
* You may want to attach a cutout of the old lady to the end of the sentence so it looks like she has actually swallowed each animal.
* Attach the names of the characters, in sequence, at the bottom of the chart to allow the children to practice matching the pictures to the words and sequencing.

74

Oh, A-Hunting We Will Go

Oh, A-hunting we will go,
A-hunting we will go.
We'll catch a _____
And put him in a _____
And then we'll let him go!

INTERACTIVE COMPONENT

* Create rhyming pairs of word cards to fill in the blank spaces in the chart. For example, *whale/pail, fox/box.*
* You can correlate this chart with the version of the rhyme *A-Hunting We Will Go* by John Langstaff.
* It is helpful to color-code the word cards by writing each pair on a different color paper. You may also want to include picture cues on the cards.

The Gingerbread Man Song

And when she mixes gingerbread
It turns into a man instead
With frosting collar 'round his throat
And raisin buttons on his coat.

(To the tune of "London Bridge")

INTERACTIVE COMPONENT

* Create word cards that children match to words in the rhyme.

ADDITIONAL SUGGESTIONS

* You can correlate this chart with *The Gingerbread Boy* by Paul Galdone.
* Attach a flannel gingerbread man to the chart. Provide flannel buttons, eyes, mouth, and nose in order for the children to create a gingerbread man as they use the chart.

A Dark, Dark Tale

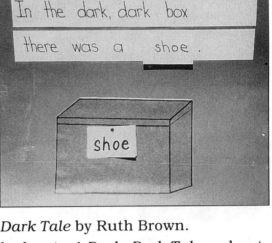

In the dark, dark box
there was a _____.

INTERACTIVE COMPONENT

⬥ Provide blank cards for children to record their predictions as to the contents of the box.

ADDITIONAL SUGGESTIONS

⬥ You can correlate this chart with *A Dark, Dark Tale* by Ruth Brown.

⬥ Cover a box with dark paper to replicate the box in *A Dark, Dark Tale* and put one item in it. The item can be a plastic mouse as it is in the book. Read the story aloud to the children and stop before the box is opened. Use the chart and the children's guesses on index cards to predict the ending. Finish reading the story and open the classroom dark box.

⬥ Change the item in the box daily. After providing some clues as to the contents, allow the children to record their predictions during free time. Open the box at the end of the day. The children especially enjoy items that they can keep, such as candy, a pencil, or stickers.

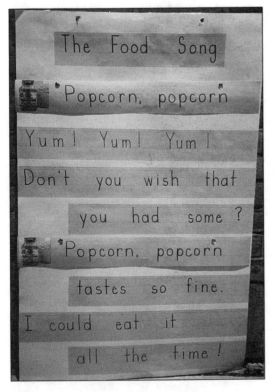

The Food Song

_____, _____
Yum! Yum! Yum!
Don't you wish that you had some?

_____, _____
tastes so fine.
I could eat it all the time!

INTERACTIVE COMPONENT

⬥ Create sets of two sentence strips for the children to fill in the blank spaces in the text.

ADDITIONAL SUGGESTIONS

⬥ You can correlate this chart with *The Very Hungry Caterpillar* by Eric Carle. Refer to the book for ideas for the food word cards.

⬥ You can also create sets of four individual word cards. As the children use the cards to fill in the blanks, they distinguish between the upper-case and lower-case initial letters.

Growing Vegetable Soup

We are growing vegetable soup
With a rake, spade and hoe.
What seeds will you plant
to help the garden grow?

INTERACTIVE COMPONENT

● Create sentence strips that the children match to the text.

● Create construction-paper flowerpots and glue them to the bottom of the chart. Glue a wooden ice cream stick in the center of each pot. Attach a paper fastener above the stick. Provide seed packets for children to hang on the paper fasteners.

ADDITIONAL SUGGESTIONS

● You can correlate this chart with the book *Growing Vegetable Soup* by Lois Ehlert. Refer to the book for choices for the seed packets.

● Depending on the level of the children, word cards can supplement or replace the seed packets.

Caps for Sale

Monkeys, monkeys
In the tree,
Throw the _____ cap
Down to me.

INTERACTIVE COMPONENT

● Create color word cards for the children to use to complete the text.

ADDITIONAL SUGGESTIONS

● You can correlate this chart with *Caps for Sale* by Esphyr Slobodkina. Refer to the book for suggestions for colors.

● To add visual interest to the chart, cut out and attach a construction-paper tree. See page 41 for reproducible monkeys that you can attach to the branches with magnetic tape.

● Provide colored caps for the children to wear to dramatize the story.

Five Little Monkeys

_____ little monkeys
jumping on the bed.
One fell off
and bumped his head.
Mama called the doctor and the doctor said,
"No more monkeys jumping on the bed!"

INTERACTIVE COMPONENT

- Create a set of cards for the number words one through five that the children change as they recite the rhyme.
- Provide a self-sticking note to cover the *s* in the word *monkeys* in the first line when appropriate.

ADDITIONAL SUGGESTIONS

- You can correlate this chart with the book *Five Little Monkeys Jumping on the Bed* by Eileen Christelow.
- Create a "Five Little Monkeys" manipulative wheel chart. See "Ten in the Bed" on page 38 for directions. Adapt those directions to make this chart.

Recommended Sources for Interactive Chart Texts

The All-Year-Long Songbook
compiled by Roslyn Rubin and
Judy Wathen
(Scholastic, 1980)

Butterscotch Dreams
by Sonja Dunn with Lou Pamenter
(Pembroke Publishers Limited Ontario,
Canada, 1987)

Chants for Children
compiled by Mary Lou Colgin
(Gryphon House, Inc., 1982)

**Circle Time Activities for
Young Children**
by Deya Brashears and Sharron Werlin
Krull
(Library Press, 1981)

**Discovering Music in
Early Childhood**
by Sally Moomaw
(Allyn and Bacon, Inc., 1984)

**Eye Winker, Tom Tinker, Chin
Chopper: Fifty Musical Fingerplays**
by Tom Glazer
(Doubleday & Co., Inc.)

Finger Rhymes
collected and illustrated by Marc Brown
(E. P. Dutton, 1980)

First Songs the Young Child Sings
by Mary Voell Jones
(Paulist Press, 1976)

Let's Make Music Today
by Mary Voell Jones
(Paraclete Publishing, 1978)

**Music for Young Americans: ABC
Series, Kindergarten Level**
by Richard C. Berg, Claudeane Burns
and Daniel S. Hooley
(American Book Company, 1963)

Pass the Poetry, Please!
by Lee Bennett Hopkins
(Harper & Row Publishers, 1987)

A Pocketful of Poems
by Mary Louise Allen
(Harper & Row Publishers, 1957)

**The Raffi Everything Grows
Songbook**
(Crown Publishers, Inc., 1989)
(A collection of songs from Raffi's album
"Everything Grows")

**The Random House Book of
Poetry for Children**
selected by Jack Prelutsky, illustrated
by Arnold Lobel
(Random House, 1983)

**Read-Aloud Rhymes for the
Very Young**
collected by Jack Prelutsky, illustrated
by Marc Brown
(Alfred A. Knopf, 1986)

A Rocket In My Pocket
compiled by Carla Withers
(Scholastic, 1990)

**September to September: Poems
for All Year Round**
by Dee Lillegard
(Children's Press, 1986)

**Sing a Song of Popcorn: Every
Child's Book of Poems**
selected by Beatrice Schenk de
Regniers, Eva Moore, Mary M. White,
and Jan Carr
(Scholastic, 1988)

**Singing and Dancing Games
for the Very Young**
by Esther L. Nelson
(Sterling Publishing Co., Inc., 1985)

Tomie dePaola's Mother Goose
(G. P. Putman's Sons, 1985)

Treasure Chest of Poetry
by Bill Martin Jr. with John
Archambault and Peggy Brogan
(DLM Teaching Resources, 1986)

Who Am I?
by Lois Raebeck
(Follett Publishing Co., 1970)

Whole Language Source Book
by Jane Baskwill and Paulette Whitman
(Scholastic, 1986)